Happily Unhappy Soul

a tale of an Ordinary Heart

Shivani Saini

BookLeaf Publishing
India | USA | UK

Made with ❤ on the BookLeaf Publishing Platform
www.bookleafpub.in
www.bookleafpub.com

Dedication

This Book is dedicated to my Bhabhi Isha Goyal and Brother Raja Paramdeep Saini who taught my heart what it is today. The amount of support and love given to me by you has given me wings to fly high and chase every dream of mine that my heart has ever desired. Your presence in my life has always been a guiding light and i am forever grateful for the bond we share. This is a small token of my gratitude, but it comes from the depths of my heart This is for you with all my heart.

Preface

In the Journey of life we dance between the lines of hope and belief. The beats of the heart are always looking for the moments joy in the delicate dance of sorrow. Happily Unhappy soul is collection of poems that reflects light on accepting each and every emotion of life which make us who we are rather then becoming the human version that others tell us to be. As Humans we are always running in life to be founded yet forgetting that the peace is in being lost. In the moment to turn out to be the strongest independent person we often forget to look around and thank the people who gave us their shoulder to cry. Each poem in this book reflects that we all are shades of grey not purely one thing or another. This Book is for those who want to embrace each emotions of life , for dreamers who have forgotten to dream and for those who accept both sides of themselves. May you find yourself reflected in these lines and may they remind you that it is okay to be both happy and unhappy sometimes all at once in your own skin.

Acknowledgements

I would like to express my special thanks of gratitude to my parents Pradeep Kumar Saini and Renu Saini who have been a source of strength in my life. A very Big thanks to my Aunty Sween Goyal for loving me so much. A heartfelt thanks to my dearest friend and sister Meenakshi sheokand for being there like a ray of sunshine in my life and always motivating me to do things that my heart loves and for loving me so much that i never forget the taste of laughter , thanks. Last but not the least a big thanks to my friends Vishakha Simran and ashima for being there for me always and forever .

1. Human's Timberland

In the moonlit stillness of Human
Timberland

the loud roar of the yellow gold
color king asked me don't you
envy my Majestic status?

i run the ministry of Dominance

i am as powerful as the sun that
rules the sky

My kingdom dances to the beats
of roar of the fierce bravery

Unlike you i don't cry tears when
sad

i hunt it down like the
timberland king

you speak of Compassion

I see it as a scent that draws the
Vultures

you sing kindness melody

but the Timberland responds to
the roar of bravery

you light the candle of sweetness

forgetting that it will be blown
away by the breeze of the night

you reflect softness as your
armor

making you prey to more yellow
gold color souls to feast on it

I conquer all the wild no doubt
no fear

even the earth feels my might

I am the Ruler of Confidence

bravest of them all

You can't match me as it takes
more than love to create a legacy.

Oh, The ruler of Timberland

did a dolphin, born, ever turn
into a shark?

But tell me, brave king, in your
fortress so stark,

2. Shadow of Silence

On an evening wrapped in the breath of frost ,
Where lonely winds whisper all that's lost,
Souls wander roads with no known end,
No love to hold, no hand to lend.
They seem at peace, but truth defies
They live beneath unspoken skies.
Each footstep echoes the shadow of silence,
A ghostly rhythm in quiet defiance.

They smile like the sun in the morning's Light
but cry inside in the still of night.
For those they love. they wear the mask,
Never daring to share or ask.
But who asks the heart if what it truly feels?
If behind bright eyes, the ache still steals?
They live each day with the shadow of silence,
A curtain drawn on their violence.

Even Kings with crowns and blazing swords,
Felt the emptiness in silent chords.

Alexander wept though the world was his,
For not all victories bring you bliss.
Arjun stood on the filed, unsure and torn,
For even glory leaves hearts worn.
Each mighty soul bore the shadow of silence,
Unseen wounds beneath the brilliance.

Oh heart of mine, so loud yet still
Do you know joy, or just the will?
Is peace a lie we long to touch?
Or something we've forgotten too much?
You beat, you burn,yet seem to hide
A storm that words have never described.
You echo always the shadow of silence,
A song unheard in emotional islands.

If we could breathe and break these chains,
Wash away these quirt stains,
Would we feel the sun inside?
Or just another place to hide?
Letting go is a scared art,
But fear grips tight the wounded heart.
Still, hope walks with the shadow of silence,
Longing to rise in vibrant defiance.

Lucky are those who learn to release,
Who dance in sorrow and find their peace

They've tasted grief, but not grown cold,
They've turned their pain into silent gold,
Their laughter is not a disguise they wear,
But a melody rising from honest prayer.
They;ve walked beside the shadow of silence,
And made of it a song of resilience.

These watery eyes reflected my truth,
The ache that's lived since early youth.
I wonder if I'll ever find
A place of rest, a quiet mind.
Is love of my own people still waiting through the haze,
To lift me from these hollow days?
Or will I always bear the shadow of silence,
A quiet ache in z world of guidance?

3. They named it Magic

When a baby arrives with a loud, sweet cry,
Two tiny stars light up every eyes.
A bundle of hope in a world so wide
They see her smile and beam with pride.
They call it magic, a gift from above,
Wrapped in innocence, laughter, and love.

She steps into life, quiet and alone.
No hand to hold, no comforting tone.
Her battles are silent, her nights are long,
Yet she learns to stand, to grow strong.
They call it magic, this growth they see,
But miss the storm she crossed silently.

The world points fingers, tears her down,
Calls her dreams a foolish crown.
Still, she builds herself through every scar,
Wishing on silence, chasing a star.
They call it magic when she won the race,
Not seeing the pain behind her grace.

She flew not to boast, but to breathe,
To escape the lies they chose to weave.
Freedom became her only desire,
So she rose alone, fueled by fire.
They call it magic, her fearless flight,
Ignoring her battles fought each night.

Now she stands where few dared tread,
Wings outstretched, past tears she shed.
They cheer her name, they sing her praise,
Blind to the fire that lit her days.
They call it magic, this woman bold
But never the story that never was told.

4. Queen of Hearts

The Queen of Hearts came knocking, soft and sweet
She whispered, :Its your love that's made this feat."
But as she reached thye door, I stood so tall,
"No" I said, "It's not just love that makes me strong at all."
For in the shadows, where the doubts may hide,
My strength came from Isha, My pillar by my side.

Then Hope arrived with promises so bright,
"You've conquered all because of your endless light."
But as her words echoed through silent air,
I answered , "No, Its not just light that led me there."
For in every step, when paths seemed hard to see
It was Isha, the Queen of hearts of my life , who believed in me.

Grief came next, with sorrow in her eyes,
"Without your tears, you'd never have reached the skies."
Yet i stood firm , my voice steady, clear,

"No, it was strength, not sorrow, that brought me here."
And through the pain, when everything seemed grim,
it was Isha's faith that lifted me within.

The Queen of hearts, with all her charms,
smiled at me, with open arms,
But at every turn, i answered each claim,
"its was not just you, or any fleeting fame"
For through the storm, through every test,
It was Isha, the Queen of Hearts, who gave me my best.

5. I wanted to built Rome

I wanted to build Rome, Brick by brick, with my own two hands,
A city of dreams, where my purpose expands.
But some roads are long and some paths are steep,
And sometimes, its Okay if our promises sleep.

I wanted to build Rome, a monument grand,
For love and for life, to stand on the land.
But love's not a tower, a palace of stone
It's moments we cherish, and not being alone.

I wanted to build Rome, a Taj for my heart,
To give something beautiful, to never depart.
But not all gifts are seen in grand, shining lights
Some gloom in the quiet, in simple delights.

I wanted to build Rome, but now I see clear,
That living is what we hold dear.
Not in surviving, but in feeling alive,
For it's how we live that lets our spirit thrive.

6. Beneath the same Stars, My brother

Beneath the same stars, my brother named Raja The King
we roam,
From your towering height to your gaze of blue,
In your quiet strength, I' ve found my guide,
Through every storm, you've stood with pride.
Beneath the same stars, you've carried the weight,
Of your silent struggles, your unspoken fate.

Beneath the same stars, my brother so bright,
Through teen years and struggles, you hid your fight.
Alone you stood, without any sign
Yet you still walked tall, taking a stand.
I never saw the burdens you bore alone,
You've given me strength, yet kept your own.

Beneath the same stars, my brother so wise,
You laugh through all phases of life, with a twinkle in
your eyes.
Your smile, it lightens up every dark place,

A warmth that's felt in your gentle embrace.
In your strength, i find courage to be,
And realize how lucky I am, to have thee.

Beneath the same stars, my Brother I see,
The life you' ve lived, the man you' ll always be.
Through all the untold hardships, you stood so tall.
Yet never once did you let me see you fall.
I was younger, yet you were always my guide,
And i wonder how you've held it all inside.

Beneath the same stars, Param the King of Isha's life
I wish for one things, as i start to weep, If i could live again, my only request
Is to have you as my brother, in every life's quest.
For your laughter, your love, your strength, so true,
Beneath the same stars, I'll always be with you.

7. A Door behind me

In Quietness of nocturne,
where the wolfs howl
a door behind me calls,
the grey the white the dark
pulling me back to the muddy ground.
through the muddy mush I slipped into the door,

The door behind me calls with a whisper so faint,
where whispers quake in shadowed halls,
Echoes of the past that time can't paint.
Thought it knocks, I must not turn around,
For in my present, my strength is found

.

The door behind me opens a dark, old wound
where the air is thick with ancient dreams,
beneath the weight of stars that weep,
A reminder of the present should not be.
But what it taught me, I choose to hold tight.
For my future's bright and the past takes flight.

.

The door behind me may try to confine
My breath a fog, the world a haze,
I tread the path of lost intent,
Lost in its shadows, some hearts intertwine.
But we're stronger now, we don't need to roam,
Living in the now, making it our home.

The door behind me may Knock once again,
But i greet today, not what has been taken away.
With open arms, I break from the chain,
Free from the past life I lived as I embrace the gain.

8. Fallen Tree

if the shadows reclaim the light they've known

can the whispering winds find their voices alone?

does a river retrace the lost banks of its flow?

can time weave the fabric of moments laid low?

have echoes forgotten their songs in the night?

does the sun greet the dawn, or flee from its light?

All these questions haunt me in the dark night

if a fallen tree would ever stand tall again

does it mean I have lost the battle to the dark of life's reign?

or does strength lie in roots that burrow deep down,

where the whispers of hope in the silence are found?

for every dusk carries the promise of dawn,

in the heart of the struggle, a new song is born.

at the depth of my deep sleep, the soul from the sky
whispered into my ears the tale of the fallen tree

once standing tall with branches wide, roots deep in
earth, with nowhere to hide.

but storms came fierce, with winds that roared, and
down it fell, its strength ignored.

yet time, the great healer being lord of gentle and wise,

breathed life again like he is the alchemist

from the gazillion broken cracks and scarred, the roots
did grow like sun glows,

for even during the hour of the loss, there is always a
room to mend the broken soul.

oh my darling butterfly, a fallen tree can always rise again; it may face the scars, battles of unloved wars, running veins of courage it learns the lesson it shall be taught.

moss grew where the shadows grow, so when you fall, my dear heart, know this truth: the life's tale of happiness waits for you like the shooting star.

in your unhappiness, find the seed of rising again; as in the shadows of dark, the stars start to glow.

for every tree that meets the ground, a forest waits to rise and surround.

in the fray of dark life, you might be lost and drift away from the seed of happiness, but remember—the hardest battles are given to the strongest.

rise, my dear star, in the dark again; though bruised and torn in the fallen ground of life, the sky gives birth to a new life.

meet me on the other side, my little star; I name you sunflower of the sky, for your story is not where you fell, but how you grew beyond it.

and so I ask, beneath these fleeting scars, can we find the
strength to embrace who we are?

will the roots entwine with love and with grace,
transforming each shadow into a warm embrace?

9. Mask of Clam

Climb the ladder, step by step, though doubt is near,
Fake it till you make it, silence all that fear.
Your heart may race, your hands may shake,
But wear a mask of clam, no cracks to break.
Even when the climb feels steep, the goal unclear,
With each brave step, you'll find your way from here.

The world will weigh you down, their judgments sharp,
When your dreams feel distant, and your light seems
dark.
Intelligent voices will say you're not enough,
But never let them see you falter or feel rough.
Put on your mask of clam, calm and serene,
And show them the strength in the spaces in between.
Let them think you're steady, even when you're not,
For they'll never know the battles you've fought.

When the journey feels endless, and your spirit wanes,

When you're tired, broken, and weighed down with pains,
The world will keep spinning, unbothered by your cries,
But wear the mask of clam, and let none see your sighs.
Even when you feel crushed, like you can't go on,
Keep that mask on your face, let your light shine strong.
For every setback is a lesson, every failure, a chance,
To grow in silence and learn to dance.

They'll try to break your will, tell you you're too small,
That you'll never rise up, you'll surely fall.
But inside, you know that your heart's made of gold,
And your dreams, though delayed, are worth more than they're told.
So wear that mask of clam, let them see your grace,
For in your silence lies a strength no one can replace.
With quiet determination, you'll rise above their doubt,
For no one can break you when you know what you're about.

10. Dear August Fairy

I met a fairy, born on August's gentle breeze,
Meeshi, her name, with a heart that aims to please.
On the 17th day, in a world full of noise,
She entered my life, and with her, came joy.
In my early twenties, we crossed paths by fate,
A friendship began, something truly great.
Why does the world forget the friends we find,
In those fleeting years that shape our mind?
The ones who turn into family, deep and true,
The ones who see us, not just through, but through and through.

At five-foot-four, she stands so small,
Yet within her heart, she holds the world's all.
Like a spark of magic, she lights up the dark,
With a soul so pure, she leaves her mark.
When I forget my worth, and the world feels cold,
She reminds me of the power within, so bold.
A sister, a guide, a beacon of light,
With her by my side, everything feels right.

She is the little sister I always dreamed,
Her love is endless, just like it seemed.
Born of God's heart, a spirit so kind,
She's the love and warmth we all long to find.
I've never met a soul so loving and true,
She loves every person, as if they are new.
Her heart knows no limits, no boundaries, no end,
She is the truest of friends, always there to mend.

In the next life, I pray we are tied,
Not just by fate, but in blood, side by side.
Meeshi, my fairy, my soul's companion,
May we walk this journey with love as our anthem.
Through every high and every low,
Our bond will flourish, and forever grow.
For in her, I found a sister, a friend,
A love that will last, a bond without end.

11. Dancing with Fear

the rhythm of life, a paradox unfolds,
while shadows whisper secrets untold.
we waltz on mountains, we stumble in streams,
each heartbeat a promise, each moment, a dream.

the echoes of laughter, the pain of goodbyes,
like shadows in twilight, beneath endless skies.
i question the stars, their shimmering glow:
do they understand love, or the depths of our woe?

beneath the bright cosmos, where dreams intertwine,
the rich and the poor dance on borrowed time.
with every heartbeat, the world shifts and sways,
we navigate fear in a daring ballet.

for love is a riddle, and life a grand stage,
we're actors en pointe, we're writing the page.
hold close the fears, let them lead you to grace,
for in every misstep, there's beauty to trace.

12. Rainbows of Opinion

in the middle of life
the rain of opinion came uninvited
yellow blue red orange
which colour did you find in life
the heart remembered when the light above sky
gives rain it does gives an umbrella with it
a shelter stitched from whispered dreams,
woven with threads of laughter and sighs,
the colors dance in puddles beneath,
reflecting hopes, as fleeting as butterflies.
let the rain fall, let it blur the lines,
each droplet a story, each splash a sign.
we paint our journey with shades of belief,
finding grace in the chaos, a moment of relief.
through storm and sun, we hold on tight,
the canvas of living, brushed with delight.
and in each downpour, we carve a way,
to dance in the deluge, to love, to sway.
embracing the mess, the beauty it weaves,
in the tapestry of life, where the heart learns to breathe.

13. Love of my life

the cold wave of air whispered
into my ears the sparkling words of life
the mirror of life showed me answers
to the language of doubts
no greater love than the self-love
not loving yourself is a sin we often commit

yet in the silence, shadows creep,
whispers of worth that we sow and reap,
in the garden of hearts, tend with care,
for beneath the surface, hope lingers there.

embrace each flaw, for they are ours,
the tangled roots that push through stars,
with every breath, let kindness prevail,
a symphony of strength in the softest exhale.

14. Escape Room

The fog in the eyes , asking me twice
have u ever tasted the run to an escape room
the left of my side beating thrice
speaking the unsaid voices of the mind
i walked down the lane of my life

a clod breez as ice
named the first lane as child
where laughter danced on the breeze,
and dreams played hide and seek with the wild.

In the shadows of echoes, whispers confide,
traces of innocence linger, now curled,
treading softly through the memories,
lost in the tapestry of a patterned world.

The fog in the eyes, a guardian of sighs,
as time weaves its stories, unseen threads,
I wander past moments, both sweet and unwise,
each step a reminder of the life that I led.

15. The Lie of Eyes

In a world where hearts are bound to hide,
We wear the mask that keeps our pain inside.
A smile so wide, yet hearts left to cry—
For the lie of eyes is where the truth must die.
We walk through the days, our faces so bright,
But beneath the surface, we struggle with night.

We shield our loved ones from the storm,
Pretending we're fine when we're far from warm.
We smile, we laugh, we make them believe,
That the hurt we feel is something we can relieve.
But in the quiet, the heart feels the weight,
And the lie of eyes speaks the unspoken fate.

Some hearts feel more than words can say,
Burdened by laughter, by sorrow, by dismay.
They absorb every glance, each whispered sound,
The kindness, the cruelty that's all around.
They carry the weight of emotions too vast,
But the lie of eyes hides the storm that's amassed.

We wear our joy like a mask for the world,
Yet inside, a different story is unfurled.

Born to feel the world in all its depth,
To carry the ache with every breath.
They carry the pain of others too near,
Too sensitive, too fragile, too full of fear.
Yet behind the smile, there's no reprieve,
For the lie of eyes is what they must weave.
We fight to stay strong, but we're barely alive,
The eyes, though they smile, they never deceive.

The soul that weeps, the heart that shatters,
Yet in the crowd, nothing ever matters.
We fake the joy, the grace, the cheer,
But the lie of eyes is crystal clear.
The world sees only what we show,
But the truth behind is something they'll never know.

So we play our part, a role so tight,
Grinning through the sorrow, hiding the fight.
We smile through the darkness, pretend to be fine,
While our eyes speak the pain that we try to confine.
The world never sees the heart's hidden cries—
For the lie of eyes is the truest disguise.
But in those silent glances, there lies a truth untold,
A story of hearts that are quietly bold.

16. World of Lost

In this world of lost, we drift and stray,
Not bound to the patterns they say we must play.
At twenty-eight, or thirty-eight, or fifty years gone,
It's okay to wonder, to feel you're not yet home.
We're taught to follow the maps that others have made,
To fit into boxes, to never be swayed.
But what if the journey is ours to define,
A path full of freedom, uniquely divine?

The questions will come, like whispers in the night,
Did I find my purpose, or is it still out of sight?
Did I fulfill what I was meant to be,
Or is there something more, something still to see?
But life isn't a road that all must tread,
It's the path we create, with each step we're led.
Each moment we wander, each choice we embrace,
Is part of the beauty in this wild race.

It's fine not to know, to feel adrift in the sea,
For the meaning of life is simply to be.

We're told it's a puzzle, a riddle to solve,
But sometimes the answers evolve as we evolve.
We don't need the answers, nor a perfect design,
In the world of lost, it's enough to be kind.
To ourselves, to the journey, to every misstep,
For in each mistake, we learn how to adapt.

So let's celebrate the failures and joys we have found,
In our own little corners, where peace can be crowned.
It's okay if we stumble, it's okay if we fall,
In the world of lost, we're all standing tall.
For in the end, what truly matters most,
Is learning to live in the world of lost.
To cherish the moments when we let go of fear,
And embrace the unknown with hope, not with tears.

In this world of lost, there's beauty in the haze,
In learning to love the uncharted maze.
So don't rush the answers, don't chase the finish line,
For the world of lost is where we'll truly shine.
Here, we create meaning with each breath we take,
And in being lost, we find all that we make.

17. The Core of my Heartbeat

The core of my heartbeat whispers soft and clear,
"Love as if there's no tomorrow, cast away your fear.
Hold nothing back, let your heart speak loud,
For love, when given freely, forms a golden shroud.
In every moment, love is born anew,
Embrace it with open arms and let it guide you through.
The world may change, but love remains the key,
A force so pure, boundless, and free."

The core of my heartbeat calls out with grace,
"Dance as if the world is a wide-open space.
Move with the rhythm of the stars and sky,
Let your feet follow your spirit, and don't ask why.
For life's too short to stand still and wait,
So dance like the music holds no fate.
When no one's watching, when no eyes can see,
It's in that freedom you find your true identity."

The core of my heartbeat speaks truth, so bold,

"Live as if your time is precious, as if you've been told,
That today is the gift, the present you hold,
And tomorrow is a story yet to unfold.
So never let worry steal your precious mind,
Live with abandon, leave doubts behind.
Each day is fleeting, a treasure to keep,
Live with passion, dive in deep."

The core of my heartbeat urges with care,
"Treat others kindly, show love, be fair.
In every soul, you'll find your reflection,
We're all part of a shared connection.
What you give is what you'll receive,
So love without fear, in others believe.
Treat them as you wish to be treated, it's true,
With kindness and compassion, your spirit will bloom
too."

Echoes of What Wasn't Asked

In the silence of a world that speaks,
The echoes of what wasn't asked begin to creep.
A woman's worth, measured by age and dress,
But no one ever asks—how does she feel, nonetheless?
From the cradle to the grave, we are shaped by their hands,
Conforming to ideals that no one understands.
The questions we didn't voice, the dreams left to die,
Are swallowed whole by the societal lie.
"Fit in, comply, follow the script,"
But they never pause to ask if our hearts are equipped.

The elders speak in tones so firm,
Demanding paths, forcing norms to squirm.
"By this age, you should settle, marry, and have a home,"
But they never ask, "Do you wish to roam?"
Their voices thunder, unwavering, sure,
But the heart longs for something pure.
They speak of duty, of legacy, of tradition's call,

Yet they never wonder if we, too, stand tall.
The echoes of what wasn't asked remain,
Whispering, "Do you wish to dance in their refrain?"
As they chart our lives with their plans and schemes,
We are left behind, chasing forgotten dreams.

They mold us to fit their ancient frame,
Chiseling us down, though we're not the same.
"Your life must follow this narrow way,"
Yet no one listens to what we wish to say.
The clothes we wear, the words we speak,
All preordained in their world so bleak.
"Be docile, be gentle, be what we expect,"
But no one asks if we can choose, or reject.
They tell us how to love, how to dress,
How to live a life of constant stress.
But where is the space to just be free,
The echo of what wasn't asked, pleading to be.
Our souls cry out, yearning for air,
But they are too busy molding us with care.

We are more than their judgments and their gaze,
More than the choices they seek to erase.
We are not their project, their canvas, their clay,
But the whispers of their norms still hold sway.
In the silence, we rise with unspoken cries,
The echoes of what wasn't asked, where truth lies.

For the heart wants what the heart desires,
And no one should silence those quiet fires.
The world may speak, and they may impose,
But deep within, the soul knows.
That the echoes of what wasn't asked will always remain,
A reminder that our true selves can't be contained.

So let us speak, let us break free,
For the echoes of what wasn't asked must be heard, you see.
The questions unasked, the dreams unspoken,
Are the seeds of the future, the bonds unbroken.
Let the silence of their demands turn to dust,
And let the voice of the soul reclaim its trust.

19. Street named alone

On the street named Alone, where shadows fall,
We learn the harsh truth, embracing the call,
In the silence, we find our strength to stand,
Life's journey is ours, no need to hold a hand.
For in the quiet of this lonely street,
We discover the power, we learn to defeat
The fears that rise when no one's around,
The solitude teaches us how to be unbound.

The street named Alone, a path we must tread,
Through joy and sorrow, the tears we shed,
No promises kept, no shoulders to lean,
Yet we walk forward, the only way we've seen.
In the darkness, we find the light within,
The courage to keep going, no matter the spin,
No one to help, no one to guide,
Yet on this road, we stand with pride.

On the street named Alone, we rise and fall,
Expectations shatter, yet we stand tall,

No one to stay, no one to leave,
In solitude, we learn to breathe.
Each step teaches us a lesson untold,
That we are both fragile and bold,
For when we walk with nothing but our own,
We realize we've always been alone.

For the street named Alone, we were born to roam,
Bound to leave, but never to be alone,
In our hearts, we build a fire,
To walk this road, and never tire.
Though the world may seem to turn away,
The street named Alone is where we'll stay,
For in the end, we are all our own,
Learning to live, to walk, to grow alone.

So walk it proud, this street so wide,
For the journey's ours, no need to hide,
On the street named Alone, we find our place,
And in our solitude, we find our grace.

20. Beyond the Fight lives Life

Beyond the noise, beyond the pain,
There's a world where love will reign.
No land, no weapon, no desire,
Can light the soul, nor quench the fire.
What is the worth of blood and stone,
When peace can reign and hearts are known?
Why fight for what will crumble fast,
When moments shared will always last?

In every heart, a hope can grow,
A seed of kindness we must sow.
Not for the gold, nor earthly fame,
But for the love that calls our name.
We're here to live, not tear apart,
To share the world and heal the heart.
For wars on earth are born of pride,
But love is where the truth resides.
To clash for power is to lose our way,
For peace is where the souls will stay.

Don't waste your time on petty strife,
For life's too short to waste in strife.
The smallest words can wound so deep,
Yet forgiveness lifts the soul from sleep.
A moment lost can never mend,
So cherish love, and never end
The bonds we share, the ones we hold,
For in them, life's true worth unfolds.
A quarrel with a friend or kin
Can rob the light that lies within.

So let us walk in harmony,
Together, strong, united, free.
No war of words, no fight of might,
Just hearts that soar and souls that light.
We're here to live, to learn, to grow,
In peace, where all our spirits flow.
For what is life, if not to care,
To lift each other, always there?
Beyond the fight, beyond the pain,
In love and peace, we'll always reign.

Let this world know, let it resound,
That joy in unity can be found.
The purpose of this life is clear:
To love each other, year by year.

So lay down arms and open hearts,
For only love will heal the scars.
We're all the same beneath the sky,
So let us live, and never die.

21. A Letter to Future

Dear Future, whatever you bring, I'm ready,
With a smile on my face, even when life feels heavy.
No matter how dark the sky may seem,
I'll stand tall, chasing every dream.
The challenges you send, I will embrace,
With grace and courage, I'll keep up the pace.
I'll face every storm, whether fierce or wild,
But my heart will stay pure, like a little child.
In a world of chaos, I'll find my peace,
Holding on to love, it will never cease.
Though you may test me with trials untold,
I'll keep my heart soft, my spirit bold.

Letter to the future, I want you to know,
That no matter how hard the winds may blow,
I will never let anger or hatred grow,
In my heart, love and care will always flow.
I may cry when harsh words are thrown,
But in those moments, I'll never be alone.

For I carry within me a strength unseen,
A love for others, pure and serene.
People may mock my tender soul,
But I'd rather be gentle than lose control.
I won't let the world's cruelty shape my core,
I'll remain kind, always wanting more.

Letter to the future, laughter may come,
From those who mock what I feel, what I've become.
But I'll choose to be the one who weeps,
Rather than break hearts or bury love so deep.
I might be soft, I might be too pure,
But kindness is something I will always endure.
I won't let harsh words make me hard,
I'll wear my sensitivity as my guard.
The world may laugh and try to tear me down,
But I'll keep my heart and wear love like a crown.
Better to cry than to become unkind,
For the heart that loves is the strongest kind.

Future, hear me when I say,
I will never walk the path where hearts decay.
I'd rather be the crybaby they scorn,
Than be the one who leaves souls torn.
With a heart full of love, I'll always stay,

I will choose compassion every single day.
I will never allow bitterness to bloom,
I'll make the world brighter, not leave it in gloom.
Though others may grow cold and turn away,
I'll keep my warmth, I'll always stay.
I'll never walk the lonely, heartless way,
I'll bring light, even on the darkest day.

So, dear future, if you break me down,
I'll still wear kindness like a crown.
Through every hardship, I'll still be true,
Loving, caring, no matter what I go through.
In a world that may choose hate, I will stand,
A heart full of love, forever unplanned.
You can challenge me, you can make me cry,
But love will always lift me high.
When the world is cold and hearts are lost,
I'll be the one to bear the cost.
And though you may try to tear me apart,
You will never change my loving heart.

This is my letter, my promise to you,
No matter what life brings, my heart will renew.
I will stay true to what I believe,
Even when the world may not perceive.
A heart filled with love, I will always defend,